THAT'S ME IN HISTORY

RENAISSANCE ITALY

Wayne L. Wilson

PURPLE TOAD
PUBLISHING

P.O. Box 631
Kennett Square, Pennsylvania 19348
www.purpletoadpublishing.com

THAT'S ME IN HISTORY

ANCIENT EGYPT
MEDIEVAL ENGLAND
MING DYNASTY CHINA
RENAISSANCE ITALY
THE SPANISH EMPIRE: THE INQUISITION

PUBLISHER'S NOTE: The data in this book has been researched in depth, and to the best of our knowledge is factual. Although every measure is taken to give an accurate account, Purple Toad Publishing makes no warranty of the accuracy of the information and is not liable for damages caused by inaccuracies.

ABOUT THE AUTHOR: Wayne L. Wilson has written numerous biographical and historical books for young adults. His most recent accomplishment is *Kate the Ghost Dog: Coping With the Loss of a Pet*. Wilson is also a novelist and screenwriter and wrote the acclaimed novel, *Soul Eyes*. He has a master's degree in education from UCLA.

Printing   1   2   3   4   5   6   7   8   9

Publisher's Cataloging-in-Publication Data
Wilson, Wayne L.
    Renaissance Italy / Wayne L. Wilson
        p. cm.—(That's me in history)
Includes bibliographic references and index.
ISBN: 978-1-62469-050-1 (library bound)
1. Renaissance—Italy—Juvenile literature.   I. Title.
 DG445 2013
 945.05—dc23
                                                    2013936506

eBook ISBN: 9781624690518

Printed by Lake Book Manufacturing, Chicago, IL

CONTENTS

INTRODUCTION

A Celebration
and a Horse Race
in Florence

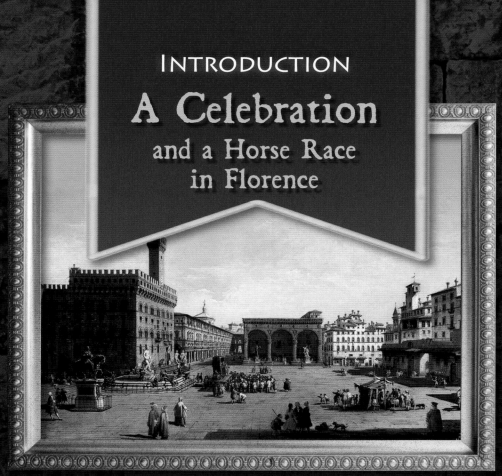

The Piazza della Signoria

The whole city is given over to revelry and feasting . . . so that this whole earth seems like a paradise.[1]

"Dance with me, Antonia, dance!" Sandra cries.

The masked street musicians are singing as a musician thumbs the strings on his pear-shaped lute. Sandra whirls around me, making me giggle. She delicately holds her plain brown dress as if it were the most lavishly flowing gown. She throws her head back causing her long hair to spill from underneath her veil. She grabs my hands and we dance and shout with glee.

Florence, Italy, is swept up in the rapture of this grand occasion. It is a hot afternoon—June 24, 1479—and we are celebrating the Feast of

The L-shaped town square, Piazza della Signoria, is filled with people talking, dancing, playing games, eating, and drinking. That towering structure behind you is our city hall, Palazzo Vecchio.

"Look, Sandra . . . in that crowd . . . those two boys wearing doublets and hoses are fighting!"

Sandra grins. "They're not really fighting. It's a sport called *civettino*.[2] The object of the game is to see who can deliver the most blows."

"Oh," I say, feeling a little silly.

Sandra is three years older than I and knows much more. I catch her gazing at the handsome boy winning the battle, but then she drops her eyes and sighs. She knows this can't become anything more than a crush.

We are servant girls and those boys are the children of noblemen.

Our thoughts are interrupted by the blasts of trumpeters marching toward us in their colorful outfits and wooly red hats. These musicians are heralding the start of a new event. They play for occasions such as the arrival of royalty, weddings, hunts, banquets, and funerals.

Listen . . . hear those snorts and whinnies? I'm getting goosebumps! Here come the horses, bearing the insignia of their owners. Their jockeys line them up at the end of the square. The race or *Palio* is about to begin! The winner's prize is a banner of crimson fabric, trimmed with fur and decorated with gold and silk. I'm sure it's worth hundreds of florins.[3]

We are servants of the richest and most powerful family in Italy— the Medici. Our master, Lorenzo de' Medici, is called "Lorenzo the Magnificent" and he loves horse racing.

Boom! The explosion of fireworks startles us. Soon, three loud bongs from the bell in the great tower of the Signoria signal the start of the race.

The horses leap forward![4] Their thunderous hooves shake the ground as they storm past, muscles glistening and rippling with every stride.

Oh no! A jockey is flung into the crowd from his wildly bucking horse, but he isn't hurt. He scrambles to his feet and chases after his horse.

After the race, come home with me and I'll share more about my life.

CHAPTER 1

Family Life and Marriage

Right now I'm on my hands and knees scrubbing the kitchen floor. I'm only nine years old and started working at the Palazzo Medici when I was seven. But age doesn't matter here. I work as hard as anyone, preparing food, sweeping, fetching water, washing clothes and hanging them to dry, scouring pots, and feeding and minding the pets in the palace.[1]

"Antonia! Stop daydreaming and hurry up! We have a big meal to prepare for the important guests arriving later."

"Yes, Ma'am," I reply, scrubbing faster.

The gray-haired woman is Tita. She's worked at the palace for over thirty years. She always says, "Antonia, be grateful the Medici family took you in. You must always work hard if you want to stay here, or you'll be back on the streets again."

She's right. My mother and I roamed the streets in bare feet and wore sackcloth to cover our bodies.[2] You'd see us in the town square or in front of the church begging for bread.[3]

Courtyard of the
Medici Palace

My father tried to farm the land, but made no money. He looked for better work in the city, but remained unemployed like so many other peasants.[4]

My mother lost two children during childbirth. I am the only survivor. It's not unusual for children, especially of the poor, to die early. Many die of starvation and disease.[5] My mother's health was always fragile. She passed away from an outbreak of the plague two years ago. I really miss her and think about her all the time.

After she died, my father hired himself out as a professional soldier, or mercenary. He said he couldn't take care of me any longer and brought me here. He said this is best for me. An older servant told me that he probably sold me to the palace for money.

The Palazzo Medici is now my *casa*,[6] or home. When I first came here, my eyes grew larger than the outdoor columns along the walkways I strolled down. It was like a dream seeing courtyards paved in stone and gardens planted with cypress and myrtle.[7]

The palace looks like a fortress from the outside and is built with crafted stone and topped with the finest cornice. It has large,

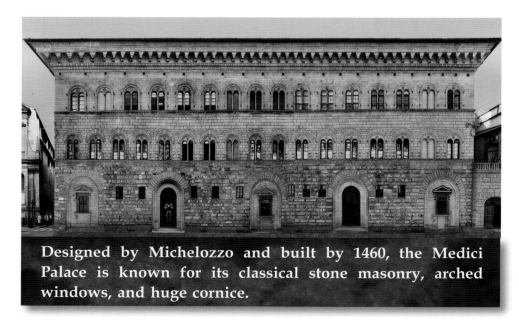

Designed by Michelozzo and built by 1460, the Medici Palace is known for its classical stone masonry, arched windows, and huge cornice.

richly-decorated, framed windows. The main entrance has grandly carved wooden doors that open onto a high-ceilinged hallway.

I gasped when I first stepped inside the palace. It was magnificent! There are colorful paintings and carved sculptures, lavish suites and offices, endless corridors, bedrooms with large canopied beds, rich fabrics draping the walls, fireplaces, fancy furniture, and a huge formal reception area.

I'm more familiar with seeing the homes of peasants and the working class. They are made of wood, earth, or stone depending on which is plentiful in the area. The roofs in these homes are usually thatched and the windows are rectangular holes with wooden shutters or oiled paper to cover them.

My family used to move all the time and sleep on dirt floors or straw beds. We would mix hay, herbs, and flowers so that when anyone would lay on the ground it masked the bad odors and made the hard ground a little softer.

Palace guests rarely see the kitchens, cellars, attics, storage facilities, icehouses, dining rooms, or servants' quarters. There are hidden passageways and service areas. One of the service wings from the main kitchen spills into a second courtyard and has its own entrance from the street. Horses go down a ramp to stables in the basement. There are rooms to store wine and oil and to make bread. Our servants' quarters are located near the basement.

The toilets are in small spaces under the stairs or close to our sleeping quarters. Drainpipes in the thick walls travel down to cesspools in the basement.[8] I like it much better than using chamber pots, like the ones my family had. Phew! I hated emptying those stinking things in the river, field, or forest.

The main kitchen the servants work in is on the ground floor so the noise, smells, and constant activity won't disturb the guests on the upper levels.

Tita supervises us, but the one who truly runs the Medici household is Mistress Clarice, wife of Master Lorenzo. Servants attending to her

Clarice Orsini

needs surround Mistress Clarice, but she is still involved in sewing, cooking, entertaining, and raising children. Women of all classes perform the duties of a housewife.[9]

I love it when we're gathered in our service quarters and Tita treats us to stories about palace events. Last night, she reminisced about Master Lorenzo's wedding to Clarice Orsini in 1469, the same year he became ruler of Florence.

Tita folded her hands and her chest heaved with a sigh as she recalled how Mistress Clarice rode into the palace on horseback, escorted by a procession of knights. Master Lorenzo handed out over a hundred calves, thousands of hens, ducks, fish, wild game, and barrels of wine to the people. Banquet tables were set up in the palace courtyard and throughout the city so Florence's citizens could join in the celebration.

Servants set the tables with rich cloths, brass bowls, silver vessels of water, silver salt cellars, forks, and knives. I never saw a fork before I came to the palace. I only ate with my hands or with a knife. Tita said that each time the servants were ready to bring in a new course of food they had to wait to be heralded by trumpet blasts. My stomach grumbled when Tita described the menu—roasts, boiled veal, mutton, pork, goat, game, beans, vegetable dishes, all kinds of spices and sauces, and wine. Best of all, for dessert there were cornets, marzipan, almonds and pine nuts, pancakes, jellies, and cakes.[10]

I'm told that the middle class, or bourgeois, dines on similar foods.

salt cellar, c. 1530

Before coming to the palace, when I did get to eat, it was mainly dark breads made of rye or barley. Like most poor peasants, my mother cooked soup with scraps of vegetables or eggs. We also ate peas, beans, pot noodles, polenta, cheese curds, and mush with grains.[11] Aristocrats cut hardened, stale bread into squares and use them as plates, or trenchers, on which to serve food. After they finish eating, the sauce-soaked bread is handed out to the poor.[12] Sometimes Mother would be lucky enough to get a piece and she would bring it home to us.

Master Lorenzo's marriage was arranged. His mother wanted her eldest son to marry a woman from a noble family to enhance their social status. This is a common practice. The church views marriage as sacred, but families also use it to strengthen business or family ties. Among the wealthy, marriages for their children are planned while they're young. It's usually sealed by a legal contract. The contract is based on the size of the woman's

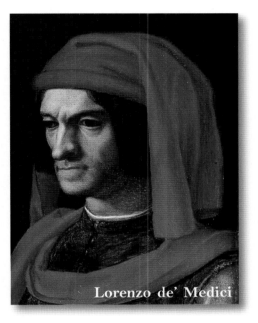

Lorenzo de' Medici

dowry, which is the money or goods her family gives to the husband. He manages all the finances and has authority over their children.[13] Women are expected to bear children and run a household. If a husband dies, the money is returned to his wife.

A poor family's dowry may only be enough to marry off one daughter. The rest are sent to a convent with a smaller dowry that helps the nuns run the convent and keeps the daughters housed and fed. Without a dowry, a woman cannot marry.[14]

I often wonder what will happen to me since I don't have a dowry. Tita told me the Medici family sometimes provides dowries to its servant girls to help them marry.[15]

THE REBIRTH OF A NEW AGE

Antonia lived in Florence during the fifteenth century, a period in which most of the population had changed very little from the Middle Ages. She probably had no idea there was a Renaissance movement underway since it mostly affected the upper class.

The Renaissance—a French word for "rebirth"—was viewed as a new age. It began in Italy and spread to the rest of Europe between 1350 and 1550. Many scholars say that Florence was the heart and living center of the era. It was a time of great cultural change and achievements in art, education, literature, science, architecture, and music.[16]

With the fall of the Roman Empire at the start of the Middle Ages, many of the advancements made by the Greeks and Romans were lost and forgotten. Near the end of the Middle Ages, the plague, known as the "Black Death," decimated the population of Western Europe and the world. People suffered through horrible living conditions, political strife, famine, and poverty.[17]

The Renaissance renewed people's interest in ancient Greek and Roman civilization.[18] Francesco Petrarch, an Italian poet and scholar of the fourteenth century, founded a philosophy called Humanism. It says people should decide for themselves how their lives should be lived, rather than relying only on answers from the Church, which they had once followed unquestioningly.

Gutenberg prints his first proof.

This major cultural movement encouraged people to learn more about philosophy—which asks deep questions about life—and classical art, literature, and science. It told them to strive for individual success.[19] Libraries of monasteries and cathedrals were often ransacked and there were excavations in cities like Rome to find old manuscripts of classic writers and relics of ancient civilizations.[20]

Another major development in the fifteenth century was the invention of the printing press in Germany by Johannes Gutenberg. He printed the first book, the *Gutenberg Bible*, which led the way for a publishing boom and more affordable books.[21] Aldus Manutius established the Aldine Press in Venice, which became the premiere printing press in Europe. In addition to other monumental works of classical literature, Manutius printed an extensive series of Greek texts written in Greek, Latin, and Hebrew.[22]

CHAPTER 2

Urban Society and the Workplace

"Close your mouth and stop staring, Antonia! You're being rude to our guest!" Tita snaps.

She carefully affixes an elaborate brooch to the lady's hair. Since the woman does not have a high forehead, Tita plucked hair from her hairline with tweezers to make her look more beautiful. The woman's hair is tied up except for a short ponytail bouncing out the back.

"Yes, Ma'am . . . I'm very sorry," I mumble, bowing my head. This gives me a chance to study the woman's *chopines*, her very high platform shoes. They are fancily decorated and the soles are made of wood. Tita once told me that the higher a woman's *chopines*, the higher her place in society. Besides being fashionable, these shoes protect the wearer from the muddy streets.[1]

"It's fine for the child to look, Tita," the woman says, chuckling. She cocks her head as she looks in the mirror, admiring the brooch Tita has pinned in her hair.

Birth of Saint John the Baptist, a Florentine fresco painted by Domenico Ghirlandaio (1449–1494), shows servants attending a wealthy, Renaissance family.

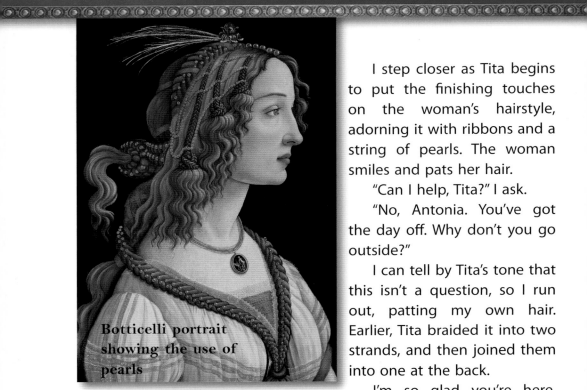

Botticelli portrait showing the use of pearls

I step closer as Tita begins to put the finishing touches on the woman's hairstyle, adorning it with ribbons and a string of pearls. The woman smiles and pats her hair.

"Can I help, Tita?" I ask.

"No, Antonia. You've got the day off. Why don't you go outside?"

I can tell by Tita's tone that this isn't a question, so I run out, patting my own hair. Earlier, Tita braided it into two strands, and then joined them into one at the back.

I'm so glad you're here. Let's go do some people watching at the Piazza della Signoria!

Look! Do you see the street performer wildly gesturing to draw a crowd? He's shouting his plans to read from a famous poem called the *Divine Comedy* by Dante, which is very popular.

Some of the rich women look so pretty in their shimmering veils and striking jewels . . . but the men can be just as vain, if not more so. Notice all the well-dressed gentlemen in their broad-brimmed hats, some covered in feathers and others trimmed with gemstones.[2]

However, most of the men in town dress in a long black gown, called a *lucco,* with a jacket underneath, and a hood or bonnet that has a ribbon hanging behind the cap.[3]

See that man wearing the sleeveless cape? Don't stare. Stay as far away from him as possible. He's a mercenary, or what some people call a cutthroat.[4] They say you can't trust them because mercenaries can be cruel and have no principles. They are only loyal to whoever pays them the most money.

It hurts to think my father may have become one.

Those stern gentlemen wearing crimson coats with ermine collars and cuffs, and briskly walking toward the Palazzo Vecchio are the *Priori*. The *Priori* are guild members elected to handle governmental duties. The Palazzo Vecchio is the home of the guilds and is the seat of the government.

The guilds run the arts and trade in Florence and are made up of the city's richest and most influential businessmen—bankers, public administrators, judges and notaries, cloth manufacturers and importers, retailers, silk merchants, and physicians. The woolen craft industry and banking houses are the main source of Florentine wealth.

But these merchants can't get rich without the help of craft guilds, which are groups of carpenters, bakers, butchers, shoemakers, blacksmiths, builders, ironworkers, girdle makers, woodworkers, innkeepers, and tanners.[5] These groups have banded together because they know there is strength in numbers. Unskilled workers are not in guilds. These include weavers, spinners, dyers, boatmen, laborers, peddlers, shepherds, soldiers, and washerwomen.

Many peasant families live in the country and work the land. Some own land, but most of it belongs to landlords and owners who charge high rent or expect a share of the harvest. A peasant's livelihood on a farm depends on things they can control, such as families working together, and things they cannot, such as the fertility of the land and the weather.[6]

Some rural people are forced to find other ways to earn a living, like making bricks, herding, woodcutting, carting material, or digging out minerals from quarries. The textile industries in wool, linen, and silk at times offer part-time work—spinning, weaving, and felting—to women in the countryside.[7]

I glance down at my shoes and feel grateful as I watch the barefoot beggars in their hole-filled garments begging for bread. When I get older, I might even earn a wage, like Tita does, instead of just room and board. For now, I feel lucky to have a full belly and a roof over my head.

THE MEDICI FAMILY: PATRONS OF THE ARTS

Antonia served in the palace of one of the most colorful and important figures in the history of the Italian Renaissance—Lorenzo the Magnificent. Like his grandfather and father, Lorenzo de' Medici ruled Florence. The name Medici comes from the Italian word *medico*, meaning medical doctor, but the Medici were not doctors. They were a banking family and grew in wealth and power throughout Renaissance Italy and Europe. The Medici were powerful citizens, but their rule never came from an elected, legal, or official status. Their power and influence came from their enormous wealth, convenient marriages, and at times by threats and payoffs to the city council. The family was also known for its generous contributions to the world of art. Lorenzo gave large sums of money and opportunities to young and talented artists to create masterworks. Some scholars say that without the Medici family's influence, there may not have been an Italian Renaissance.

The Medici patronage of artworks began with Giovanni di Bicci de' Medici, the great grandfather of Lorenzo. He commissioned an architect named Filippo Brunelleschi to reconstruct the Basilica di San Lorenzo in Florence.[8] In the early fifteenth century, Giovanni married a beautiful noblewoman from a wealthy and respected Florentine family. He also founded the Medici Bank. His business boomed when the popes in Rome used the bank, which helped his family become one of the richest in Europe.[9]

Giovanni's son, Cosimo de' Medici, used the wealth he inherited from his father to increase his political power. An important patron of the arts, he gave money to many artists and created the modern Platonic Academy in Florence, where men gathered to discuss the

Adoration of the Magi, painted by Leonardo da Vinci, shows how some artists of the period were paid to include members of the Medici family in their paintings, as the onlookers here include Giovanni, Cosimo, Piero, and Giovanni's grandsons Giuliano and Lorenzo de' Medici.

important ideas put forth by the Greek philosopher Plato. Cosimo also built the Palazzo Medici.[10]

Cosimo died in 1464 and was succeeded by his son, Piero I. Piero continued the family's tradition of contributing to the arts, buying Dutch and Flemish artworks and collecting rare books. Unfortunately, he struggled through many health issues and died of gout and lung disease after five years of rule.

Piero's son Lorenzo was only twenty years old when he became the ruler of Florence.[11] The Medici's love of art pushed Florence into the center of the Italian Renaissance and inspired other city-states to support their own artists.

CHAPTER 3

Church and the Religious Way of Life

I'm sure you're wondering about those men dressed in costumes, carrying staffs and knapsacks, and wearing caps with scallop shells.

They are called pilgrims, and they've devoted their lives to God. Pilgrims travel to faraway places in search of shrines and holy lands. A pilgrim's journey to Rome takes place on old, dusty, rock-strewn roads that wind through the mountains. Sometimes they face cold rain and harsh winds. It's not only bad weather they encounter; bandits and mercenaries often hide in the hilltops and castles, waiting to rob them.[1]

You can always find a place to worship in Florence. There are shrines everywhere. Worshipers usually leave candles or flowers, especially when they're praying to the Virgin Mary for help.

Vittore Carpaccio,
Pilgrims Meet the Pope

It's common to see monks and nuns in the city. Nuns cut their hair short and wear veils and robes called habits. Monks wear robes, caps, and strange haircuts called tonsures in which their hair is shaved in a circle off the tops of their heads but left in a ring below. It looks as if they're wearing crowns made of hair. The wool robes of the monks and nuns are colorless and dull.[2] They make sacrifices in their appearance to assure God that they have given up all forms of vanity and dedicated their lives to the church. Monks live in monasteries and nuns live in convents.

See that little boy running through the streets, hoisting a skull on a stick? That's a message warning us of damnation if we don't repent our sins. Many of these preachers claim that we are going to Hell because of our vanity and loving ourselves more than God. They say that anything that tempts us to sin must be destroyed. I often hear them raging about a terrible book called the *Decameron* by a writer named Boccaccio. They say it leads people to do sinful acts because of its stories of love.

Be careful if you decide to listen to a wandering friar in his outdoor pulpit screaming about the abuses of the Roman Catholic Church and the Pope. I've seen townspeople get so upset that they burn books, paintings with nude figures, wigs, jewelry, hair combs, and even fake teeth! Anything that may tempt us to sin or think impure thoughts is thrown into the fire. They call such a fire a "bonfire of the vanities."[3]

Tita warned me that the friars are false prophets and messengers of the Devil. When I hear them ranting, I leave right away. I love Jesus. I want salvation so I can be with Him in Heaven, where a person can eat whatever she wants all day long and she never has to scrub a dirty floor.

Florence has many lovely chapels and cathedrals. They're full of captivating stained glass windows, paintings, and frescoes, which are murals painted on walls and ceilings. People also worship at home, setting up devotional holy images of Christ, the saints, and the Virgin and Child. Strings of beads called rosaries are also popular in our society and are used to keep track of the number of prayers we've said.[4]

Look straight up! That's the pointed dome of the cathedral Santa Maria del Fiore. We call it the *Duomo*. I once overheard Master Lorenzo telling someone that *duomo* comes from the Latin phrase *domus Dei,* which means "house of God." You can learn a lot tiptoeing around a palace where wise people live. The dome part was built in 1436. Isn't it one of the biggest structures you've ever seen? The Master told his guests that an architect named Filippo Brunelleschi designed it and that it contains more than four million bricks. Here's something I figured out for myself—you can see the Florence Cathedral's dome from just about anywhere in the city.[5]

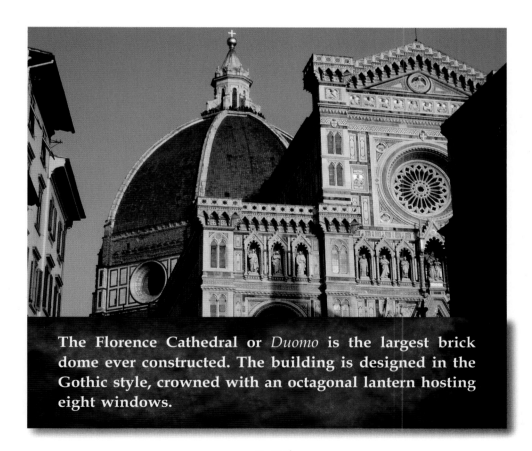

The Florence Cathedral or *Duomo* is the largest brick dome ever constructed. The building is designed in the Gothic style, crowned with an octagonal lantern hosting eight windows.

LEONARDO DA VINCI AND THE SCIENTIFIC REVOLUTION

Leonard da Vinci was truly a Renaissance man. He was a painter, inventor, sculptor, architect, scientist, musician, engineer, botanist, and more. If there ever was a person who could be described as a genius who could see into the future, it would be Leonardo. He created designs for flying machines, a tank, a submarine, a parachute, machine guns, an armored car, a calculator, and solar power hundreds of years before they came into existence.

Leonardo di ser Piero da Vinci was born in 1452 to a notary, Piero da Vinci, and a peasant woman, Caterina, at Vinci in Florence. It was quite common for people during this period to receive the surname of the region where they were born. At the age of fourteen, Leonardo served as an apprentice to one of the most famous artists in Florence, Andrea di Cione, known as Verrocchio, who immediately recognized Leonardo's colossal talent. Verrocchio's workshop profoundly influenced Leonardo's creative development and work. Verrocchio was an excellent teacher and in his workshop Leonardo was exposed to a wide range of technical and artistic skills, such as drafting, chemistry, metalworking, drawing, painting, and sculpting. Leonardo spent a great deal of time studying with Verrocchio and collaborated with him on many of his artistic works including his painting of the *Baptism of Christ*.

In 1478, Leonardo's first major commission was to paint an altarpiece for the Chapel of St. Bernard in the Palazzo Vecchio. In 1481, he painted *Adoration of the Magi* for the monks at San Donato a Scopeto.[6]

Lorenzo de' Medici hired Leonardo to construct a silver lyre, which is a type of harp, in the shape of a horse's head. In 1482, Da Vinci

The Last Supper,
Lenoardo da Vinci

presented it to Ludovico Sforza, Duke of Milan, as a gesture of peace. Thereafter, Leonardo spent seventeen years in the service of the duke as a military engineer. He also produced drawings and paintings including *The Last Supper*. Upon his return to Florence, he created his most famous painting, the mysterious *Mona Lisa*, sometime between 1503 and 1506.[7]

Leonardo was fascinated by human anatomy. He dissected cadavers, or dead bodies, and created detailed sketches of body parts. Uncomfortable with this practice, Pope Leo X banned him from Rome's mortuary, where the deceased were kept.[8]

Da Vinci's impressive notebooks were filled with designs for military weapons such as crossbows, catapults, cannons, armored vehicles, flying machines, fortresses, a tank, a machine gun, and a submarine.[9] The notebooks also contained a remarkable amount of animal movements, plant growth, maps, astronomy, the first telescope design, and more.[10]

CHAPTER 4

War and Politics

"Despots!"

"Tyrants!"

"No one elected them! The Medici made themselves rulers of our city! They have all the money and all the power, and we, the peasants, have none!"

I cautiously walk past a small bristling group of people in the street in front of the palace. They are gathered around a man I cannot see, but his bellowing voice makes him sound as if he's ten feet tall.

I feel a lot of tension in the air as I nervously glance at the palace guards in their dark yellow caps, yellow-and-white striped sleeves, black armor plates, and the crest of the Medici. You would think that as a servant in the House of the Medici I would be used to the guards by now, but I am still afraid of them. The stone-faced guards monitor the crowd from their positions in front of the palace. I doubt they plan on breaking up the gathering crowd unless the people become unruly. The Medici

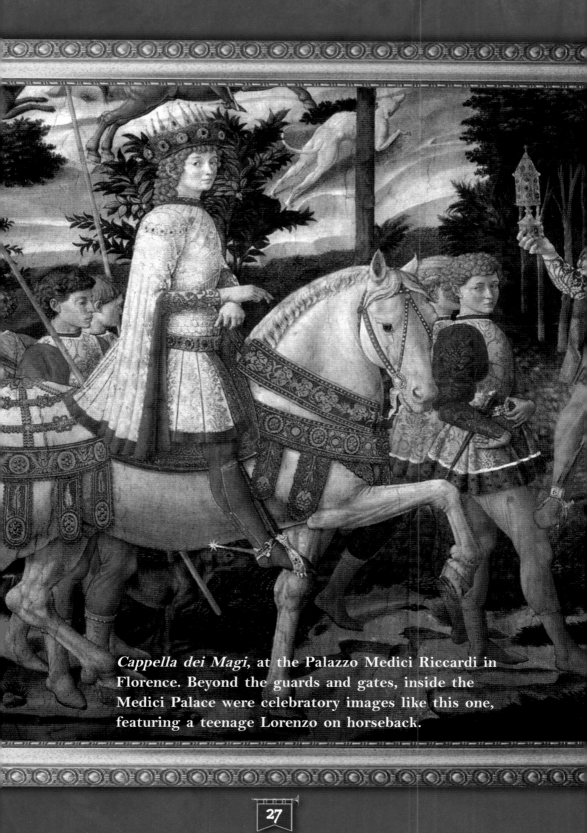

Cappella dei Magi, at the Palazzo Medici Riccardi in Florence. Beyond the guards and gates, inside the Medici Palace were celebratory images like this one, featuring a teenage Lorenzo on horseback.

are beloved by most citizens; yet, beyond the celebrations, there are jealousies and swirling tensions.

I know this because I hear people talking. I don't understand politics, and I may not be very wise, but I'm a good listener. I remember walking in the town square one very cold morning and overhearing two elderly

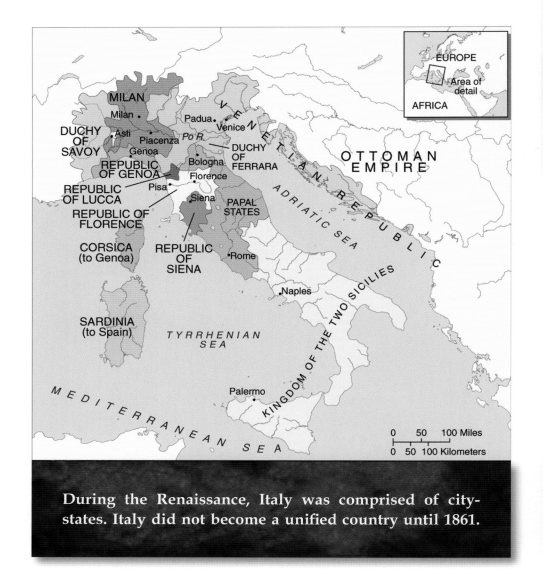

During the Renaissance, Italy was comprised of city-states. Italy did not become a unified country until 1861.

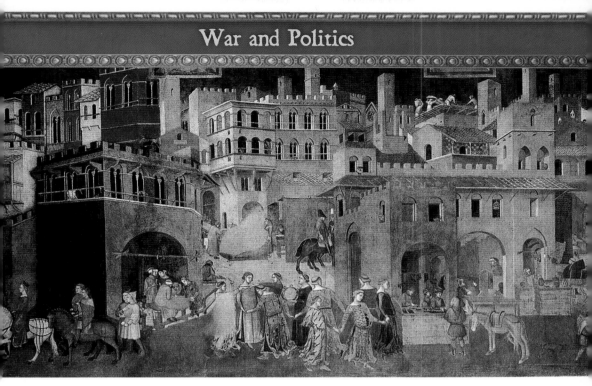

The streets were alive with talk and ideas during the Renaissance.

men in a heated debate. They were both wearing coats that looked too large for them, mainly because of the shoulder pads inside their coats. I crept up and stood near them, curious as to what they were arguing about. One of the men glanced at me, but quickly ignored me when his friend said something that made him roll his eyes in frustration. Perhaps if I had been a guard they would have reduced their voices to a whisper, but since I'm only a servant girl, they continued to argue loudly.

"Matteo, I am telling you, my grandparents used to tell me how in ancient Roman times we were united as a people, we spoke in one voice, and shared a common heritage. I wish I had lived back then instead of now. In today's society we are divided. We formed into different city-states and territories. We speak different languages, the government no longer serves the people . . . everyone finds something to shout about, but nobody listens."[1]

"Oh, Carlo, stop being ridiculous! No country has *ever* spoken in one voice! People are naturally different. Most of us may agree on some issues, but there will always be ones who disagree. That's not going to change. Yes, there may have been peaceful times in those days, but I'm sure there were smaller battles going on and war was lurking around the corner then just like it is now."

"You are so negative. We are not at war today!"

"Maybe not today, Carlo, but what about tomorrow? Our history has shown that there has been constant warfare between the city-states for years. On land and sea, they have vied for power, control, and territorial expansion. These battles have allowed the larger and more powerful city-states to take over their smaller neighbors.[2] Venice, Milan, the Papal States, Naples, and, fortunately, our beautiful Florence have emerged as the most powerful ones.[3]

The man named Carlo sighed and shrugged his shoulders. "Matteo, I can't argue with that, but thankfully, in 1454 we all agreed to the Peace of Lodi, which so far has prevented outbreaks of war."[4]

"Yes, but again I ask you, Carlo, will peace still hold until tomorrow?"

The Battle of Cascina, **painted by Michelangelo, celebrates the Florentine victory over bitter rival, Pisa, on July 28, 1364.**

Giuliano de' Medici is fatally stabbed by assassins in the *Duomo*. His brother Lorenzo manages to escape.

That's when I walked away . . . fearful of Carlo's reply. It only reminded me of the bad things that happened not long ago. Last year, there was an evil plot to overthrow the Medici as rulers of Florence by killing them. The plot was cooked up by their jealous business rivals, the Pazzi family, and other enemies. The assault occurred at the *Duomo* on April 26, 1478. It was Easter Sunday, during High Mass. Master Lorenzo and his brother, Giuliano, were viciously attacked. There was much confusion, chaos, and screaming as people fled in every direction. I couldn't see anything because Tita shielded me with her body, but I heard every horrible detail of what happened later when the other servants whispered the story over and over. Master Giuliano was stabbed many times and died right on the cathedral floor. Master Lorenzo fought back, before escaping with a stab wound in his neck.[5] An enraged mob chased and caught many of the conspirators and brutally killed them. Some were hanged from the windows of the Palazzo della Signoria.

Ever since the attack, I sometimes wake up in tears from nightmares. Every night I pray with all my heart that we will remain in peace.

THE LITERATURE OF THE TIMES

Niccolò Machiavelli

Diplomat, philosopher, historian, politician, and author, Machiavelli was born in 1469. His books include the *Discourses on the First Decade of Titus Livius*, *Art of War,* and *History of Florence and of the Affairs of Italy*—his first book, *The Prince,* is his masterpiece. This political tale reflects Machiavelli's years of service as an ambassador and is a guide on how to get and keep political power. Banned by the Pope, *The Prince* became a handbook for tyrants and dictators.[6]

Giovanni Boccaccio

Boccaccio was an author, poet, and scholar. Born in 1313, his greatest work is the *Decameron*. The story is set in 1348 during the time of the Black Death in Florence. Ten young women and men flee from the horrors of the plague in the city and live in an abandoned country villa in which in ten days they tell one hundred stories about love.[7]

Baldassare Castiglione

Castiglione is best known for his popular and influential *The Book of the Courtier*. The book is a series of evening conversations between Court of Urbino members who try to describe how a gentleman and lady should act in a cultured society.[8] It's been used as a guide on manners for the nobility and middle class and was the most widely distributed book of the sixteenth century.

Giovanni Pico della Mirandola

Humanist, philosopher, and writer, Pico passionately believed in free will and man's unlimited potential. When he settled for a time in Florence in 1484, he met Lorenzo de' Medici who became one of the most influential people in his life. Until his death in 1492, Lorenzo supported and protected Pico, who died two years later. While in his early twenties, Pico challenged all to debate him in Rome on his 900 religious and philosophical theses. Pico's best-known work is his *Oration on the Dignity of Man*, often referred to as the "Manifesto of the Renaissance."[9]

CHAPTER 5

Renaissance Creativity and Art

Art is as plentiful in Florence as the air we breathe. Come and see the bronze statue of David in the courtyard of Master Lorenzo de' Medici's palace. I heard the artist Donatello carved it over half a century ago. There it is in the center of the courtyard, on top of that column, nearly life-size. Look at the smile on his young pretty face as he nonchalantly stands bearing the sword of Goliath at his side, with his foot resting on the giant's severed head. The antique gems carved on Goliath's helmet are exquisite.[1] Some people are uncomfortable when they see David naked except for his helmet and boots. I find him beautiful. In our society, it's not uncommon to see nude figures in paintings, sculptures, and other forms of art.

Next, we are going to visit the private chapel of the Medici family. I am so excited to show you the chapel that I can feel myself

Donatello's *David*

Built around 1444 by Cosimo the Elder, the Medici Chapel, or Chapel of the Magi, is famous for its series of wall paintings by Benozzo Gozzoli.

trembling. It is on the first floor of the palace. I think you will love it . . . it is *so* beautiful!

Now that we're inside the chapel, don't you feel like you need to shield your eyes because of the marble floors that shine like the sun? Tita told me that the famous artist Benozzo Gozzoli decorated the chapel years ago. He painted striking frescoes showing the Procession of the Magi to Bethlehem. Look around and you'll see that the Procession occupies three walls of the main room in the chapel. See the shepherds awaiting the announcement of the Infant Jesus, the angels in adoration, and the magi, or kings? The frescoes are so vivid, you can almost imagine you're part of the procession. They direct us to the very end of the room and the end of our journey. There, encircled by those benches, on that raised altar, is a painting of the *Adoration of the Magi*.[2]

Like me, I'm sure you'd like to stay in this wonderful chapel forever and be surrounded by this blessed art, but we have to leave before I get in trouble. It's okay . . . I want to show you something that's incredible—how art can adorn something unexpected—like a door or a tomb. We've got to hurry and catch Gasparo, who is one of the cooks, before he drives his cart into town. Otherwise we'll have to walk!

"Thank you, Gasparo!"

"You're welcome, Antonia." He yanks on the ropes for the oxen to pull to a stop. "Be careful as you step out of the wagon. And watch out for all the droppings on the street."

"We will. Goodbye!"

Gasparo is right. These streets are filled with droppings from oxen, horses, dogs, cats, birds, and rats. Even with all the beautiful buildings around us, the streets are rarely clean.

I see you brushing off all the dust on your clothes. I don't blame you. Whew. Hopefully we don't smell like oxen after taking that long wagon ride.

Hey, do you recognize that building over there? You're right, that's the *Duomo*! And in front of us is the Baptistry of St. John where everyone in the city has been baptized for centuries.[3]

"What else do you know about the baptistry?"

The voice seems to rise out of nowhere. Suddenly a young man stands up, carrying a large sketchpad with a partially finished design of the baptistry. My eyes immediately find a connection with the ground as I begin toying with my single braid.

"I don't know . . . " I answer, hearing the shyness in my voice. "My friend and I just came to look at it because it's one of the prettiest buildings in the city."

"True," says the young man. "But it's most famous for its gilded bronze doors with relief sculptures designed and created by Lorenzo Ghiberti. The relief sculptures were finished in 1424 after twenty-one years. The process involved modeling, casting, gilding, and finishing. The east door is the most popular with its twenty-eight decorative

The bronze doors of the Baptistry of St. John

panels—twenty depict the life of Christ and the other eight depict four evangelists and four saints.[4]

"Wow. You sure know a lot about it."

"I should. My name is Alfonso and I'm an apprentice to one of the artists in Florence. And I'm going to be very famous one day just like Ghiberti," he boasts. "I've studied this building for a long time. Do you like my sketch?" He holds it up.

"It's very nice," I reply, raising my eyes and then lowering them quickly.

"Have you ever been inside?"

Embarrassment sweeps over me. "No, but I'm going to be baptized there someday."

I can feel Alfonso studying me. Suddenly I wish we could run away, but then his brash tone softens.

"Well, you don't have to wait for that. Come on . . . I'll take both of you inside."

"You will?" I find it hard to contain my excitement.

"Sure. Follow me."

The first thing Alfonso shows us is the marble and bronze tomb of Baldassare Cossa, Antipope John XXIII.

"Donatello and Bartolomeo, the designers of the Palazzo Medici, created this tomb. Look at the richness of detail rendered on Cossa's resting body above the inscription on the stone coffin. If you look overhead you'll see the Madonna and Child.[5] The female figures below with the *aureole*, or radiant light, behind them are the three virtues of salvation—Faith, Hope, and Charity. And don't you love how that magnificent canopy frames it all?"

"Yes I do," I say, gazing in awe at the tomb.

After the tour is over, Alfonso escorts us out of the baptistry. "Well, I better complete my task for the day and get back to my sketch. I hope I didn't bore you folks."

"No, no, not at all," I say quickly. "Thank you so much. Good luck on your art!"

"Thanks. And good luck to you and your friend," Alfonso says, sitting cross-legged on the ground in front of the baptistry and resuming his sketching.

Wow! He turned out to be a really nice person. Maybe one day we'll see each other again. Before we go back, I'd like you to see how a certain type of art can be created. The place I'm taking you to is a short walk from here. Let's go.

This is my friend, Jacopo. He is a carpenter and an apprentice to his father, but he also paints frescoes in Florence. He promised to tell us a little bit about the process.

"*Buonasera*, Antonia, and good day to your friend as well. The first things you must do in painting a fresco are to carefully prepare the wall's surface and put up the right type of scaffolding so you can reach high places. If you work outside, be aware of the weather. If it's cold and wet, the plaster will not dry; and if it's too hot, then it may dry before the section is completed. If the weather is right, I begin work by laying on a rough layer of plaster.

Next, I quickly sketch in an underdrawing. Once I place a fresh patch of fine, wet plaster on a small section, the painting begins. Oh, before I forget, I always start my work at the ceiling and the top of the wall.[6]

That's all for now, Antonia. I better get back to work before the paint dries."

"And I better return to the palace before Tita starts looking for me. Thank you, Jacopo. *Ciao!*"

Famous Artists, Sculptors, Architects, and Musicians

Donatello

Florentine sculptor Donatello was born in 1386. His most highly regarded work is *David*, the first freestanding, nude bronze figure sculpted since the Roman era. He is also lauded for *Gattamelata*, the first statue of a soldier on horseback standing in a public place since ancient times.[7]

Lorenzo Ghiberti

Born in Florence in 1378, Ghiberti was a sculptor, architect, and artist. He is most highly praised for his masterful craftsmanship of the bronze doors for the Baptistry of the Florence Cathedral. The final pair is referred to as the "Doors of Paradise."[8]

Raphael

One of the greatest painters of the Renaissance era, Raphael was born in Urbino, Italy, in 1483, and died at the age of 37. He is best-known for his series of *Madonna* paintings in the Vatican. One of his most famous frescoes is *The School of Athens*.[9]

Michelangelo

Born in 1475, Michelangelo was once a protégé of Lorenzo de' Medici and lived in the palace.[10] He went on to become one of the world's greatest artists. His most famous works are the *Pieta* and *David* statues and the magnificent ceiling frescoes of Rome's Sistine Chapel.[11]

Palestrina

Palestrina is the most celebrated member of the sixteenth century Roman school of musical composition. His style of smooth, balanced, and harmonic polyphony (for two or more melodic voices) strongly influenced the development of music in the Roman Catholic Church. In his lifetime, Palestrina wrote hundreds of sacred music compositions.[12]

476	The Roman Empire falls.
500–1500	Europe experiences the Middle Ages.
1348–1350	The Black Death ravages Europe. Florence suffers a major loss in population. The total number of people is reduced from 120,000 in 1338 to 50,000 in 1351.
1351–1355	Boccaccio completes the *Decameron*. Venice is defeated by Genoa.
1374	Petrarch dies. Boccaccio dies a year later in 1375.
1380	Venice defeats Genoa and becomes the ruler of Levantine trade.
1397	The Medici Bank is founded in Florence.
1401	Lorenzo Ghiberti is awarded a commission to create doors for the Baptistery of San Giovanni in Florence.
1403	Brunelleschi and Donatello travel to Rome to study ancient ruins.
1417	Brunelleschi designs the dome for the Florence Cathedral.
1420	The Papacy moves back to Rome.
1434	Cosimo de' Medici's thirty-year rule of Florence begins.
1440–1442	Donatello sculpts *David,* the first freestanding statue made since antiquity.
1446	Brunelleschi dies.
1447	Pope Nicholas V founds the Vatican Library.
1450	Francesco Sforza conquers Milan and becomes duke.
1452	Leonardo da Vinci is born.
1454	The Peace of Lodi establishes peace between major powers in Italy. The Gutenberg Bible is published. The printing press revolutionizes European literacy.
1459	Benozzo Gozzoli paints *Adoration of the Magi.*
1469	Lorenzo de' Medici takes power in Florence.
1471	Sixtus IV becomes Pope and turns the papal states into a strong dominion.
1478	The Pazzi conspiracy fails to overthrow the Medici in Florence.
1483–1486	Pico is declared a heretic because of his *900 Treatises,* but is protected by the Medici. He writes *Oration on the Dignity of Man* in 1486.
1490	Aldus Manutius establishes the Aldine Press in Venice.
1492	Lorenzo de' Medici dies.
1494–1498	The Medici are expelled from Florence. Radical Friar Girolamo Savonarola takes power in Florence from 1494–1497. Savonarola is burned at the stake for heresy in 1498. Leonardo da Vinci paints *The Last Supper* from 1495 to 1498.
1503–1505	Da Vinci paints the *Mona Lisa*. Michelangelo completes his statue of *David*.
1508	Michelangelo paints the ceiling of the Sistine Chapel.
1510–1511	Raphael paints *The School of Athens.*
1512	The Medici regain control of Florence.
1513	Machiavelli writes *The Prince*. Lorenzo de' Medici's son becomes Pope Leo X.
1519	Da Vinci dies.
1527	Rome is sacked by troops of the Holy Roman Empire. The Medici are driven from Florence once again.
1528	Castiglione's *The Book of the Courtier* is published.
1535	The death of Francesco II brings Milan under Spanish rule.
1541	*The Last Judgment* is painted by Michelangelo.
1650–1700	Europe experiences the Age of Enlightenment.

Introduction: A Celebration and a Horse Race in Florence

1. John R. Hale, *Renaissance* (New York: Time Inc., 1965), p. 150.
2. Ibid., p. 155.
3. J. Lucas-Dubreton, translated by A. Lytton Sells, *Daily Life in Florence: In the Time of the Medici* (New York: The Macmillan Company, 1961), p. 132.
4. Ibid.

Chapter One: Family Life and Marriage

1. Elizabeth S. Cohen and Thomas V. Cohen, *Daily Life in Renaissance Italy* (Westport: Greenwood Press, 2001), p. 192.
2. Jill Condra, ed., *The Greenwood Encyclopedia of Clothing Through World History* (Westport: Greenwood Press, 2008), p. 50.
3. Peter Burke, *Culture and Society in Renaissance Italy, 1420–1540* (New York: Charles Scribner's Sons, 1972), p. 240.
4. John R. Hale, *Renaissance* (New York: Time Inc., 1965), p. 37.
5. Thinkquest, "Children in the Renaissance", http://library.thinkquest.org/C006522/life/children.php
6. Marta Ajmar-Wollheim and Flora Dennis, eds., *At Home In Renaissance Italy* (London: V & A Publications, 2006), p. 77.
7. John R. Hale, *Renaissance,* (New York: Time Inc., 1965), p. 89.
8. Marta Ajmar-Wollheim and Flora Dennis, eds., *At Home In Renaissance Italy* (London: V & A Publications, 2006), pp. 35–37.
9. Ibid., pp. 151–154.
10. Francesco Da Mosto, *Francesco's Italy* (London: BBC Books, 2006), pp. 84–86.
11. Ducksters, "Renaissance Food," http://ducksters.com/history/renaissance_food.php
12. Eras of Elegance: "The Renaissance Era (1450–1600)," http://erasofelegance.com/history/renaissance life.html
13. Victoria and Albert Museum (article), "Women in the Renaissance", http://www.vam.ac.uk/content/articles/w/women-in-the-renaissance/
14. Evelyn Welch, *Art and Society in Italy 1350–1500* (New York: Oxford University Press, 1997), p. 282.
15. Elizabeth S. Cohen and Thomas V. Cohen, *Daily Life in Renaissance Italy* (Westport: Greenwood Press, 2001), p. 203.
16. Mark Kishlansky, Patrick Geary, and Patricia O'Brian, *Civilization in the West,* http://wps.ablongman.com/long_kishlansky_cw_6/35/9178/2349794.cw/index.html
17. John R. Hale, *Renaissance* (New York: Time Inc., 1965), pp. 13–14.
18. Ibid., pp. 15–16.
19. The Humanism of the Renaissance, http://www.all-about-renaissance-faires.com/renaissance_info/renaissance_and_humanism.htm
20. John R. Hale, *Renaissance,* (New York: Time Inc., 1965), p. 24.
21. Steven Kreis, "The History Guide: The Printing Press", http://www.historyguide.org/intellect/press.html
22. Margaret L. King, *The Renaissance In Europe* (London: Laurence King Publishing Ltd., 2003), p. 92.

Chapter Two: Urban Society and the Workplace

1. Renaissance Dress Glossary, http://aneafiles.webs.com/glossary.html
2. Renaissance Spell, "Renaissance Fashion," http://renaissance-spell.com/Renaissance-Fashion.html
3. J. Lucas-Dubreton, translated by A. Lytton Sells, *Daily Life in Florence: In the Time of the Medici* (New York: The Macmillan Company, 1961), p. 124.
4. Ibid., p. 125.
5. John R. Hale, *Renaissance,* (New York: Time Inc., 1965), p. 78.
6. Elizabeth S. Cohen and Thomas V. Cohen, *Daily Life in Renaissance Italy* (Westport: Greenwood Press, 2001), p. 24.
7. Ibid., p. 26.
8. John T. Paoletti and Gary M. Radke, *Art In Renaissance Italy* (New York: Harry N. Abrams, Inc., 1997), pp. 187–188.
9. Lauro Martines, *April Blood: Florence and the Plot Against the Medici* (New York: Oxford University Press, 2003), p. 38.

10. Evelyn Welch, *Art and Society in Italy 1350–1500* (New York: Oxford University Press, 1997), pp. 289–291.
11. John T. Paoletti and Gary M. Radke, *Art In Renaissance Italy* (New York: Harry N. Abrams, Inc., 1997), p. 294.

Chapter Three: Church and the Religious Way of Life
1. John R. Hale, *Renaissance,* (New York: Time Inc., 1965), pp. 50–51.
2. Jill Condra, ed., *The Greenwood Encyclopedia of Clothing Through World History* (Westport: Greenwood Press, 2008), p. 148.
3. John R. Hale, *Renaissance,* (New York: Time Inc., 1965), p. 66.
4. Marta Ajmar-Wollheim and Flora Dennis, eds., *At Home In Renaissance Italy* (London: V & A Publications, 2006), pp. 192–196.
5. John T. Paoletti and Gary M. Radke, *Art In Renaissance Italy* (New York: Harry N. Abrams, Inc., 1997), p. 189.
7. Ibid., pp. 295–297.
8. Leonardo da Vinci Biography, http://www.biography.com/people/leonardo-da-vinci-40396
9. John R. Hale, *Renaissance,* (New York: Time Inc., 1965), p. 130.
10. John T. Paoletti and Gary M. Radke, *Art In Renaissance Italy* (New York: Harry N. Abrams, Inc., 1997), p. 317.

Chapter Four: War and Politics
1. John T. Paoletti and Gary M. Radke, *Art In Renaissance Italy* (New York: Harry N. Abrams, Inc., 1997), p. 42.
2. Evelyn Welch, *Art and Society in Italy 1350–1500* (New York: Oxford University Press, 1997), pp. 27–28.
3. John R. Hale, *Renaissance,* (New York: Time Inc., 1965), p. 34.
4. History World, History of Italy, "The Peace of Lodi: AD 1454–1494," http://www.historyworld.net/wrldhis/PlainTextHistories.asp?ParagraphID=hlh
5. Miles J. Unger, *Magnifico: The Brilliant Life and Violent Times of Lorenzo De' Medici* (New York: Simon & Schuster, 2008), pp. 313–314.
6. J. R. Hale, *Machiavelli and Renaissance Italy* (New York: The Macmillan Company, 1960), p. 3.
7. William Rose Benét, *The Reader's Encyclopedia,* 2nd ed., (New York: Thomas Y. Crowell Company, 1965), pp. 614, 816.
8. Ibid., p. 257.
9. Alison Cole, *Virtue and Magnificence: Art of the Italian Renaissance Courts* (New York: Harry N. Abrams, Inc., 1995), pp. 171–173.

Chapter Five: Renaissance Creativity and Art
1. John T. Paoletti and Gary M. Radke, *Art In Renaissance Italy* (New York: Harry N. Abrams, Inc., 1997), p. 229.
2. Ibid., p. 227.
3. Martin Wackernagel, *The World of the Florentine Renaissance Artist: Projects and Patrons, Workshop and Art Market,* translated by Alison Luchs, (Princeton: Princeton University Press, 1981), p. 21.
4. John T. Paoletti and Gary M. Radke, *Art In Renaissance Italy* (New York: Harry N. Abrams, Inc., 1997), pp. 177–178.
5. Evelyn Welch, *Art and Society in Italy 1350–1500* (New York: Oxford University Press, 1997), pp. 96–97.
6. Ibid., pp. 66–67.
7. John T. Paoletti and Gary M. Radke, *Art In Renaissance Italy* (New York: Harry N. Abrams, Inc., 1997), p. 267.
8. Mario Monteverdi, ed., *Italian Art to 1850* (New York: Grolier, Inc., 1965), pp. 73–74.
9. Ibid., pp. 135–139.
10. Patricia Lee Rubin, *Images And Identity In Fifteenth-Century Florence* (New Haven: Yale University Press, 2007) p. 166.
11. Walter Paatz, *The Arts of the Italian Renaissance: Painting, Sculpture, Architecture* (New York: Harry N. Abrams, Inc., 1974), pp. 28–29.
12. Palestrina, Encyclopedia Britannica, http://www.britannica.com/EBchecked/topic/439795/Giovanni-Pierluigi-da-Palestrina

Books

Avery, Catherine B., ed. *The New Century Italian Renaissance Encyclopedia*. New York: Appleton-Century-Crofts, 1972.

Brown, Patricia Fortini. *Art and Life in Renaissance Venice*. New York: Harry N. Abrams, Inc., 1997.

Burckhardt, Jacob. *The Civilization of the Renaissance in Italy*. New York: The Modern Library, 1954.

Connor, James A. *The Last Judgment*. New York: Palgrave Mamillan, 2009.

Klein, Stefan. *Leonardo's Legacy: How Da Vinci Reimagined the World*. Cambridge, MA: Da Capo Press, 2010.

Lev, Elizabeth. *The Tigress of Forli*. Boston: Houghton Mifflin Harcourt, 2011.

Nava, Simonetta. *Painting in Renaissance Italy*. New York: Rizzoli, 1999.

Olson, Roberta J. M. *Italian Renaissance Sculpture*. New York: Thames and Hudson, 1992.

Parks, Tim. *Medici Money: Banking, Metaphysics, and Art in Fifteenth-Century Florence*. New York: W. W. Norton & Company, 2005.

Weinstein, Donald. *Savonarola: The Rise and Fall of A Renaissance Prophet*. New Haven: Yale University Press, 2011.

Works Consulted

Ajmar-Wollheim, and Flora Dennis, eds. *At Home In Renaissance Italy*. London: V & A Publications, 2006.

Burke, Peter. *Culture and Society in Renaissance Italy, 1420–1540*. New York: Charles Scribner's Sons, 1972.

Cohen, Elizabeth S., and Thomas V. Cohen. *Daily Life in Renaissance Italy*. Westport: Greenwood Press, 2001.

Cole, Alison. *Virtue and Magnificence: Art of the Italian Renaissance Courts*. New York: Harry N. Abrams, Inc., 1995.

Condra, Jill, ed. *The Greenwood Encyclopedia of Clothing Through World History*. Westport: Greenwood Press, 2008.

Da Mosto, Francesco. *Francesco's Italy*. London: BBC Books, 2006.

Hale, John R. *Renaissance*. New York: Time Inc., 1965.

Hale, J. R. *Machiavelli and Renaissance Italy*. New York: The Macmillan Company, 1960.

King, Margaret L. *The Renaissance In Europe*. London: Laurence King Publishing Ltd., 2003.

Lucas-Dubreton, J. Translated by A. Lytton Sells. *Daily Life in Florence: In the Time of the Medici*. New York: The MacMillan Company, 1961.

Martines, Lauro. *April Blood: Florence and the Plot Against the Medici*. New York: Oxford University Press, 2003.

Monteverdi, Mario, ed. *Italian Art to 1850*. New York: Grolier, Inc., 1965.

Paatz, Walter. *The Arts of the Italian Renaissance: Painting, Sculpture, Architecture*. New York: Harry N. Abrams, Inc., 1974.

Paoletti, John T., and Gary M. Radke. *Art In Renaissance Italy*. New York: Harry N. Abrams, Inc., 1997.

Rubin, Patricia Lee, and Alison Wright. *Renaissance Florence: The Art of the 1470s.* London: National Gallery Publications Ltd., 1999.

Rubin, Patricia Lee, *Images and Identity in Fifteenth-Century Florence.* New Haven: Yale University Press, 2007.

Unger, Miles J. *Magnifico: The Brilliant Life and Violent Times of Lorenzo De' Medici.* New York: Simon & Schuster.

Wackernagel, Martin. Translated by Alison Luchs. *The World of the Florentine Renaissance Artist: Projects and Patrons, Workshop and Art Market.* Princeton, Princeton University Press, 1981.

Welch, Evelyn. *Art and Society in Italy 1350–1500.* New York: Oxford University Press, 1997.

On the Internet

Ducksters: Renaissance Food
http://ducksters.com/history/renaissance_food.php

Focus on Florence
http://learner.org/interactives/renaissance/florence.html

History World: "History of Florence"
http://www.historyworld.net/wrldhis/plaintexthistories.asp?historyid=aa69

The Humanism of the Renaissance
http://www.all-about-renaissance-faires.com/renaissance_info/renaissance_and_humanism.htm#

The Italian Renaissance
http://www.historydoctor.net/Advanced%20Placement%20European%20History/Notes/italian_renaissance.htm

Leonardo da Vinci Biography
http://www.biography.com/people/leonardo-da-vinci-40396

Renaissance Dress Glossary
http://aneafiles.webs.com/glossary.html

Renaissance Spell: "Renaissance Fashion"
http://renaissance-spell.com/Renaissance-Fashion.html

"The Rise of the Merchant Classes—The Medici Family"
http://www.skwirk.com.au/p-c_s-56_u-422_t-1105_c-4273/WA/7/The-rise-of-the-merchant-classes-the-Medici-family/Renaissance-in-Europe/Renaissance-and-Reformation/SOSE-History/

Sarah Bradford Landau, "Renaissance (1300s–1600s)"
http://www.scholastic.com/browse/article.jsp?id=3753904

Sparknotes: "Women in the Renaissance"
http://www.sparknotes.com/history/european/renaissance1/section9.rhtml

annex—To add territory by conquest or occupation.

antipope—One who makes a significantly accepted claim to be Pope in opposition to the Pope already elected.

aristocrat—A member of the ruling class or of the nobility.

bourgeois—A person that belongs to the middle class.

city-state—An independent state consisting of a city and surrounding territory.

conspiracy—An agreement to perform an illegal, wrongful, or sinister act.

courtier—A person who is in attendance at the court of a king or other royal personage. One who often seeks favors, especially by insincere flattery.

diplomat—A person often appointed by a nation who is skilled in the art and practice of conducting negotiations between countries without arousing hostility.

doublet—A man's close-fitting jacket that is shaped and fitted to his body. It is usually hip- or waist-length and worn over the shirt or drawers.

dowry—Money, goods, or estate that a woman brings to a marriage.

florin—Gold coin that originated in Florence.

fresco—The art of painting on freshly spread moist plaster with water-based pigments.

guild—An association of individuals with similar goals and pursuits to control the arts and trades in their town.

hose—Style of men's clothing for the legs and lower body. During the 15th century, hoses were fitted to the leg and often multicolored, usually with a color for each leg.

lyre—A stringed instrument similar to a harp having two curved arms connected at the upper end by a cross bar. It was used by the ancient Greeks to accompany songs or to recite poetry.

mercenary—One who serves or works primarily for monetary or material gain. A professional soldier hired for service in a foreign army.

peasant—A person who is either a laborer or owner of a small farm; an uneducated person of a lower social class.

pilgrim—A religious devotee who embarks on a quest to journey to a shrine or holy place.

plague—A horribly contagious disease that can be widespread and cause a high rate of death.

saint—Officially recognized by the Catholic Church for having an exceptional degree of holiness and believed to be in Heaven.

shrine—A place or sanctuary where religious devotion is paid to a saint or deity.

town crier—A town officer who makes public proclamations as required by the court.

$ 29.95